0

zero

cero

10

ten

diez

20

twenty

veinte

30

thirty

treinta

40

forty

cuarenta

50

fifty

cincuenta

60

sixty

sesenta

70

seventy

setenta

80

eigthy

ochenta

90

ninety

noventa

100

one hundred

cien

1000

one thousand

mil

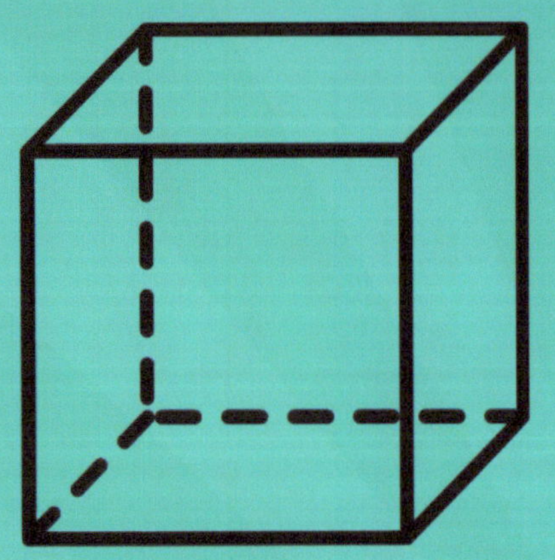

cube

cubo

block

bloque de juguete

ice cube

cubo de hielo

caramel

caramelo

sugar

azúcar

dice

dados

gift box

caja de regalo

cardboard box

caja de cartón

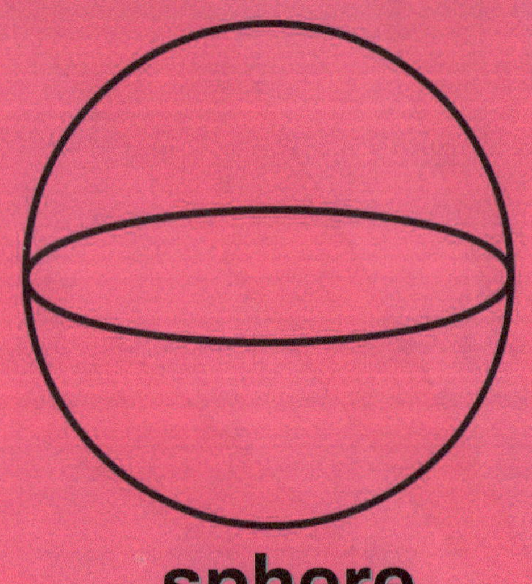

sphere

esfera

ice cream scoop

cuchara para helado

pearl

perla

bubble

burbuja

marbles

canicas

planet

planeta

snowball

bola de nieve

tennis ball

pelota de tenis

cylinder

cilindro

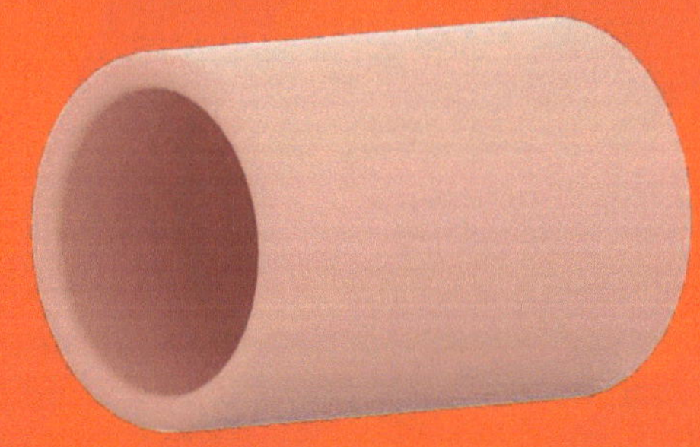

tube

tubo

batteries

baterías

thread spool

carrete de hilo

cinnamon

canela

rolling pin

rodillo

sausage

salchicha

hay bale

paca de heno

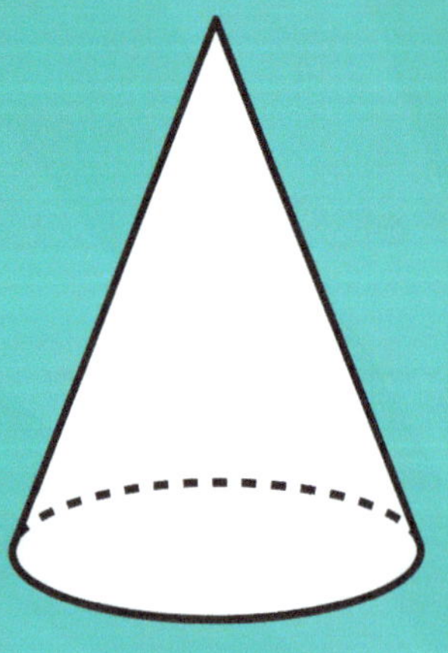

cone

cono

road cone

cono de tráfico

ice cream cone

cono de helado

witch hat

sombrero de bruja

dungeon

mazmorra

fir tree

abeto

party hat

sombrero de fiesta

snail

caracol

blackberry

mora

currant

grosella

clementine

clementina

durian

durián

dragon fruit

fruta del dragón

jackfruit

yaca

star fruit

carambola

asparagus

espárragos

radish

rábano

red bean

frijol rojo

turnip

nabo

cassava

mandioca

sweet potato

ñame

chickpeas

garbanzos

eagle

águila

bat

murciélago

beaver

castor

flamingo

flamenco

raven

cuervo

blackbird

mirlo

blue tit

herrerillo azul

magpie

urraca

swallow bird

golondrina

lark

alondra

parakeet

periquito

woodpecker

pájaro carpintero

peacock

pavo real

parrot

loro

toucan

tucán

stork

cigüeña

coral

coral marino

sea anemone

anémona de mar

sea urchin

erizo de mar

seahorse

caballito de mar

clownfish

pez payaso

goldfish

pez dorado

crab

cangrejo

hermit crab

cangrejo ermitaño

dolphin

delfín

narwhal

narval

octopus

pulpo

squid

calamar

whale shark

tiburón ballena

orca

orca

blue whale

ballena azul

beluga whale

ballena beluga

hammerhead shark

tiburón martillo

white shark

tiburón blanco

lemon shark

tiburón limón

tiger shark

tiburón tigre

grasshopper

saltamontes

caterpillar

oruga

scorpion

escorpión

lizard

lagarto

dinosaurs

dinosaurios

black hair

pelo negro

ginger hair

pelirrojo

brown hair

pelo castaño

blond hair

pelo rubio

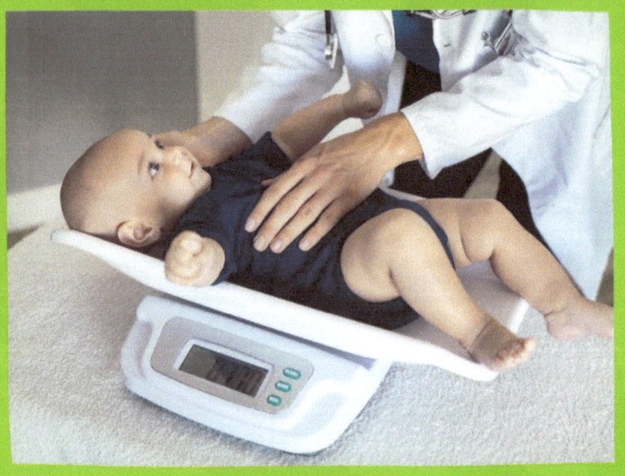

scale

báscula

hospital

hospital

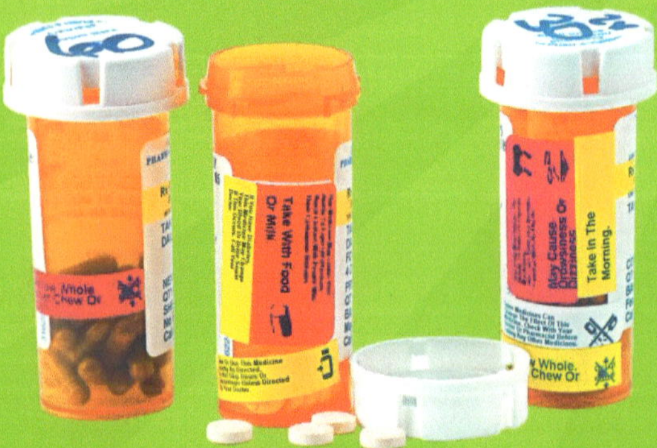

medicine

medicina

thermometer

termómetro

bandage

vendaje

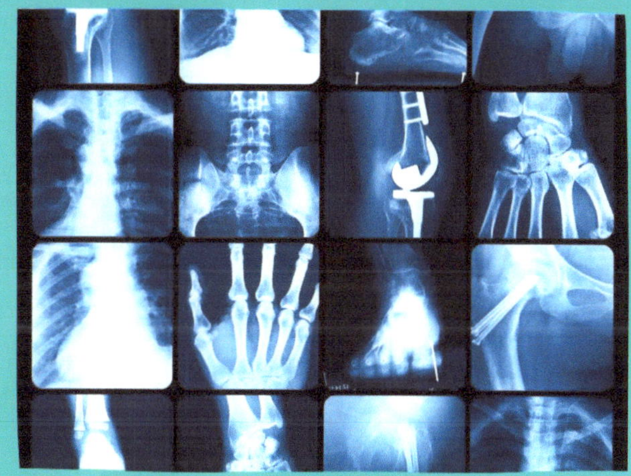

x-ray

radiografía

doctor

doctor

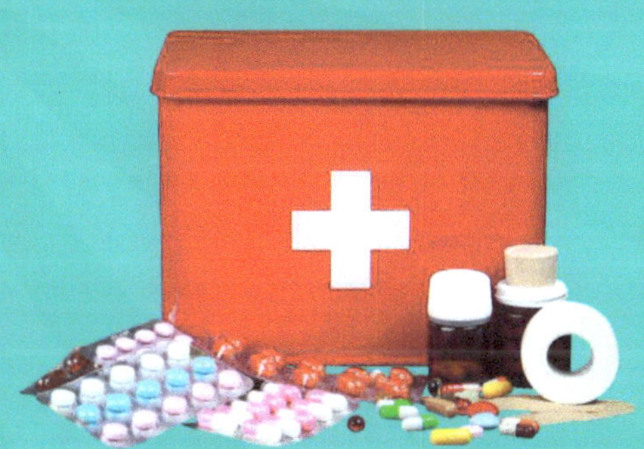

first aid kit

kit de primeros auxilios

play

jugar

draw

dibujar

count

contar

write

escribir

dancing

baile

swimming

natación

skiing

esquí

basketball

baloncesto

tennis

tenis

ping pong

ping pong

soccer

fútbol

horse riding

equitación

ice hockey

hockey sobre hielo

judo

judo

boxing

boxeo

running

carrera

baseball

béisbol

cricket

grillo

rugby

rugby

volleyball

voleibol

maracas

maracas

tambourine

pandereta

xylophone

xilófono

violin

violín

piano

piano

guitar

guitarra

cello

violonchelo

harp

arpa

drum

tambor

djembe

djembé

drum kit

batería

trumpet

trompeta

horn

trompa

saxophone

saxofón

flute

flauta

headphone

auriculares

sing

cantar

sheet music

partitura

microphone

micrófono